...with...

Abraham Lincoln

A U.S. President Biography Book for Kids

Written by Bobby Basil

3 FREE BOOKS!

Hi! I'm Alex!

I'm nine, and I don't know
what I want to be
when I grow up.

There are so many
amazing things to do!

My mom helps me text with
important people and ask them
questions about their lives.

It's fun to ask questions!

Today my mom and I are
texting with...

Abraham Lincoln!

Abraham Lincoln was the
16th U.S. President and
lived from 1809 to 1865.

He led the United States
through the Civil War and
ended slavery in the U.S.

I can't wait to text him
my questions!

Hi Abraham!

Hi Alex!

Thank you for texting with me.

You're welcome.

What do you look like?

I look like this...

Where were you born?

I was born in a one room log cabin in Sinking Spring Farm, Kentucky.

Your house only had one room?!

Yes. That's how many people lived in the 1800s.

I guess that's kind of like how people are living in tiny homes now.

What is a tiny home?

It's a very small house that people can drive around with a car. But it has electricity and running water and everything.

That sounds very fancy. We did not have electricity, running water, or even a bathroom in my log cabin.

Wow. That's a hard way to grow up.

It was. When I was seven, my family moved to Indiana. Two years later, my mom passed away.

I'm sorry to hear that.

Thank you. My father married another woman, and she became my stepmother.

Did you like her?

Yes. We became very close.

That's good.

Sometimes it's tough liking a new person, especially if they are becoming your new parent.

You should always be open to new people in your life. Things might change with the new person, but that could be good.

Did you go to school as a kid?

I mostly taught myself. I had less than a year of teaching from school.

Less than a year is not a long time!

I worked on my father's farm, and there wasn't a school nearby. I did not like the physical work of farming, but I always loved to read.

I love to read, too!

Reading is wonderful. You can learn many things about the world by reading. I read so much on the farm that people would call me lazy.

That's not nice for people to call you lazy.

My life's path was not to work on a farm. When I was twenty one, my family moved to Illinois.

You moved a lot growing up!

I did. A few years later, I ran for public office in Illinois.

Did you win?

No, I lost. But I did not give up. I kept reading and learning and ran again. And then I won!

That's great!

I served four terms in the Illinois House of Representatives. I also became a lawyer and started practicing law.

You had two jobs at the same time?!

Both jobs were very important to helping my country improve. I led many legal cases, and I appeared before the Illinois Supreme Court 175 times.

In trials, I argued for what was fair, and people began to call me "Honest Abe."

I like that nickname! When I texted with Amelia Earhart, I nicknamed myself Treasure Map.

That's also a good nickname.

So how did you go from being a lawyer to being President?

In 1858, Stephen Douglas was running for re-election as Ilinois' senator. I ran against him and we had many important debates.

What is a debate?

It's where two people argue in favor or against something.

That's kind of like what you were doing as a lawyer!

Exactly! At this time in American history, more states were being added to the country. Some of the new states were "free" states but some allowed slavery.

I don't understand why America allowed slavery. It's one of the worst things in the world.

I agree.

At one of the debates with Stephen Douglas, I gave a famous speech about the future of America.

What did you say?

A house divided against itself cannot stand. I believe this government cannot endure permanently half slave and half free.

So you were saying that something had to change in America?

Yes I was. Remember how my stepmother turned out to be a good change?

Yes.

It was painful for my mother to pass away, but out of that came a good change.

And that's what the Civil War was? Painful but good in the end?

It needed to happen.

Our country could not continue half slave and half free.

Did you win the election against Stephen Douglas?

No. But because I lost, I was able to run for President two years later and I won.

Yay! That was another bad thing that turned out to be good.

Yes. Sometimes a painful loss is a blessing in disguise.

So how did the Civil War start?

Once I was elected President, southern states that allowed slavery began to leave, or secede, from the United States.

But the country is called the UNITED States!

The southern states did not think so.

I said it was illegal to secede from the Union, When The South fired shots on Fort Sumter, I declared war.

That must have been a tough decision.

It was. And the Civil War was very long and violent. In the end, the Union won and we preserved the United States of America. Also during my presidency, Congress passed the 13th Amendment, which ended slavery.

That's good!

But how did you treat the southern states that left the Union?

With forgiveness. Even when you are angry, you need to forgive people or nothing with change for the better.

Thank you for the advice!

You're welcome!

It was fun talking to
Abraham Lincoln!

I think I want to
learn more about
U.S. Presidents now.

There are a lot more
Presidents
that I can text
to learn more.

I can't wait to text
the next one!

FUN QUESTIONS FOR YOU FROM . . .
ABRAHAM LINCOLN
WRITE YOUR ANSWERS IN THE TEXTING BUBBLES!

How many rooms are in your home?

What is something you thought was bad that turned out to be good?

Who have you forgiven?

COMPARE AND CONTRAST WITH . . .
ABRAHAM LINCOLN

How are you and Abraham the same?

_____

_____

_____

_____

How are you and Abraham different?

_____

_____

_____

_____

THINKING ABOUT THE LIFE OF . . .
ABRAHAM LINCOLN

How did Abraham's life make you feel?

_____

_____

_____

_____

Would you want to live a day in Abraham's life?
Why or why not?

_____

_____

_____

_____

LEARNING FROM . . .
ABRAHAM LINCOLN

What did you find most interesting about Abraham's life?

_____

_____

_____

_____

What did Abraham teach you?

_____

_____

_____

_____

WHAT FIVE W QUESTIONS WOULD YOU TEXT ABRAHAM LINCOLN?

1. Who _____ ?

2. What _____ ?

3. When _____ ?

4. Where _____ ?

5. Why _____ ?

meme Time WiTH . . .
ABRAHAM LINCOLN

DRAW A PICTURE THAT DESCRIBES
ABRAHAM LINCOLN'S LIFE!

"Whatever you are, be a good one."

- Abraham Lincoln

"The best way to predict your future is to create it."

- Abraham Lincoln

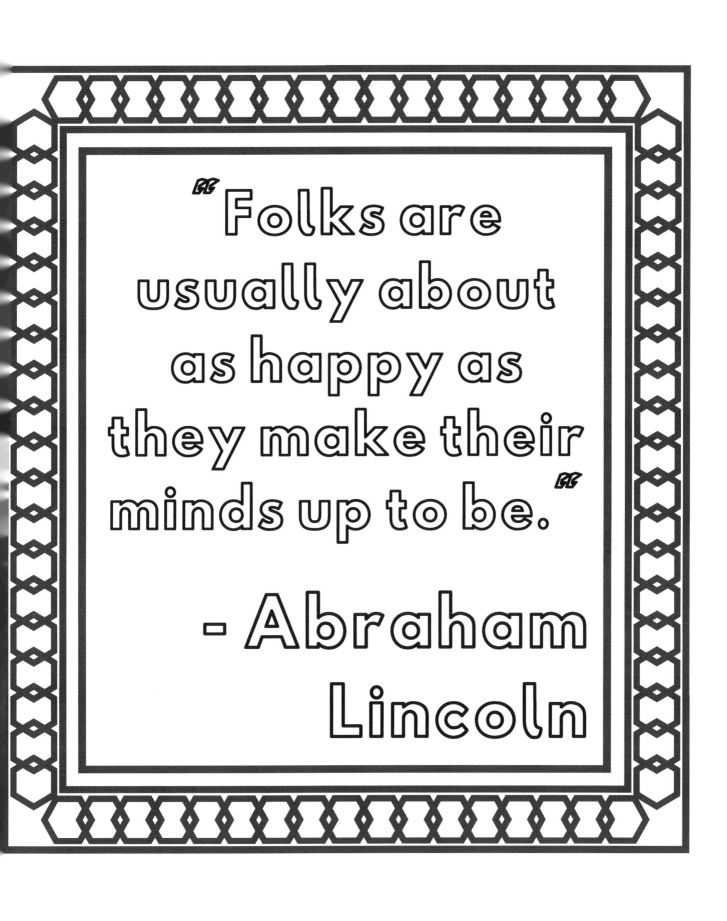

PLEASE
LEAVE A REVIEW
ON AMAZON!

Your review will help other readers discover my books. Thank you!

Made in the USA
Las Vegas, NV
15 November 2020